SCIENCE TOPICS

Forces & Motion

PETER RILEY

Heinemann
LIBRARY

First published in Great Britain by Heinemann Library,
Halley Court, Jordan Hill, Oxford OX2 8EJ,
a division of Reed Educational and Professional Publishing Ltd.

Heinemann is a registered trademark of Reed Educational & Professional
Publishing Limited.

OXFORD MELBOURNE AUCKLAND
JOHANNESBURG BLANTYRE GABORONE
IBADAN PORTSMOUTH NH (USA) CHICAGO

Designed by AMR
Illustrations by Art Construction and Jon Davis
Printed in Hong Kong

04 03 02 01 00
10 9 8 7 6 5 4 3 2 1

ISBN 0 431 07662 6
This title is also available in a hardback library edition (ISBN 0 431 07668 5)

British Library Cataloguing in Publication Data
Riley, Peter D.
Forces and motion. – (Science topics)
1.Force and energy – Juvenile literature 2.Motion – Juvenile literature
I.Title
531.1·1

Acknowledgements
The Publishers would like to thank the following for permission to reproduce photographs:
Action Plus pgs 4 /Phillippe Millereau, 11(b), 16, 20 /Glyn Kirk, 15(t) /Chris Barry, 19 /Richard
Francis; B & C Alexander pg 21; J Allan Cash pgs 7, 17, 23(b), 27, 28; John Cleare/Mountain
Camera pg 15(b); FLPA/Lee Rue/Images of Nature pg 9(b); Science Photo Library pgs 5 /Jerry
Lodriguss, 6 /Julian Baum, 24 /Martyn F. Chillmaid, 25 /Alex Bartel, 26 /Bruce Iverson, 29; Frank
Spooner Pictures pgs 9(t) /Sydney Freelance, 12 /Brock Peter/Liason, 13 /Burrow/Liason; The
Stock Market, pgs 18, 23 (t) /Brownie Harris; Telegraph Colour Library/FPG International pg 11(t).

Cover photograph reproduced with permission of Action-Plus Photographic.

Our thanks to Jane Taylor for her comments in the preparation of this book.

For more information about Heinemann Library books, or to order, please phone 01865 888066, or
send a fax to 01865 314091. You can visit our web site at www.heinemann.co.uk

Any words appearing in the text in bold, **like this**, are explained in the Glossary.

Contents

What is a force?

A **force** is a push or a pull which usually produces **motion** (movement). When something is in motion it is moving. A force can make a stationary object start moving. It can make a moving object change direction, speed up, slow down or stop. A force can also make an object change its shape.

SCIENCE ESSENTIALS

A force is a push or a pull.
Your **weight** is due to the pull of **gravity**.
A force acts in one direction. Forces occur in pairs. Each one acts in the opposite direction to the other. The pairs of forces may be balanced or unbalanced.

How your body pushes and pulls

You can soon identify where forces act if you think about the movements you feel and see in your daily life. For example, the first force you may be aware of in the day is the pull of the muscles on your eyelids. Other forces that follow may be the pulling forces of arm and leg muscles on your bones. The muscles make your arms push your body out of bed and make your legs push you up into a standing position. From then on your body exerts pushing and pulling forces on all kinds of things as you get washed, dressed, have breakfast and prepare for the rest of the day. Think about these forces when you get up tomorrow.

Weight – your personal force

Your body pushes down on the ground with a force called weight. This force is due to the pull of gravity on the substances that make up your muscles, bones, brain and other organs in your body.

The forces acting on these cars send them in different directions and change their shape!

Pairs of forces

When a force acts in one direction, there is a second force that acts in the opposite direction. This means that forces always act in pairs. When the strength of a force acting in one direction is matched by the strength of a force acting in the opposite direction, the forces are balanced and there is no movement. Just close this book and press on its front and back covers with each hand with the same force and the book will stay still. Now, push slightly harder with one hand and see how the book changes position. If the strength of one force changes, the forces no longer balance and movement takes place.

How still are you?

You may not think you are moving as you read these words, but your eye muscles will have pulled your eyes to the right and left as you read this sentence. In your wrist and neck your **pulse** is throbbing at a rate of more than once per second as your heart beats inside your chest to push blood round your body.

Your whole body and surroundings are moving at a few hundred kilometres per hour as the Earth spins on its axis. You are moving in other directions, too, because the Earth is moving around the Sun, and the Sun and its planets are moving around the centre of the **Milky Way** (our Galaxy). The Earth is pulled round the Sun by the force of gravity (see page 26). This same force pulls the **Solar System** round the Milky Way. Nothing in the **Universe** is still. Even the galaxies are moving apart – scientists believe that this is the result of an explosion, called the Big Bang, which formed the Universe 15 billion years ago. All these movements in the Universe, both large and small, take place because of the push or pull of a force.

▶ Thousands of millions of stars are moving around the centre of this galaxy, pulled by the force of gravity.

5

Gravity in the Universe

There is a **force** of attraction between any two objects in the **Universe**. This force is called **gravity**. Its effects can only be seen or felt when one object is very large (like the Earth) and the other object is very much smaller (like you), or if the two objects are both very large (like the Sun and the Earth). A very large object like the Earth has a gravitational force field around it. This is a region around the object where gravity pulls on other objects. We live in the Earth's **gravitational force field** and see and feel its effects every moment of our lives. There are gravitational force fields around other large objects in the Universe, too, and the force fields of some of them affect conditions on Earth.

SCIENCE ESSENTIALS

A force of attraction exists between any two objects in the Universe. This force is called gravity.
Gravity weakens with increasing distance from a planet, **moon** or **star**. It holds the planets in their **orbits** in the **Solar System**, causes the **tides** in the Earth's oceans and holds light inside a **black hole**.

The strongest pull of gravity

When certain stars finish shining, they eventually collapse. If a star over three times more massive than the Sun collapses, it forms an object with such a strong force of gravity that even light — the fastest thing in the Universe — cannot escape. This object is called a black hole. Its strong force of gravity pulls material out of any nearby star.

◄ Material from the star on the left has been pulled away by the gravitational pull of the black hole. The material is swirling round the black hole before it is finally drawn into it.

How gravity weakens

As you move away from a large object like the Earth, its gravitational pull becomes weaker. A fast-moving aircraft flying 10 kilometres above the Earth would be pulled back to Earth if its jet engine were switched off, but a fast-moving space shuttle flying at over a thousand kilometres above the Earth would be pulled round the planet in a path called an orbit if its engines were off. A spacecraft further out in space could pass the Earth without being pulled by Earth's force of gravity at all.

The grip of gravity

The Sun is more than a million times bigger than the Earth and its strong force of gravity holds the planets in their orbits in the Solar System. Most of the planets have at least one moon. A moon moves in orbit around a planet, pulled by the force of gravity that exists between them.

Sun, Moon and tides

Our Moon's gravitational force pulls on the surface of the Earth. This does not affect the land, but the pull on the oceans creates two bulges in the water on opposite sides of the planet. As the Earth rotates, the bulges move across its ocean surfaces and create high and low tides on the seashore. Twice a month the Sun, Earth and Moon are in line as the Moon orbits the Earth. At these times the pull of the Sun's gravity adds to the pull of the Moon's gravity, causing bigger than usual high and low tides, called spring tides.

▶ The gravitational force between the Moon and the Earth will pull the water down this beach.

Measuring forces

A force, such as **gravity**, can be measured with an elastic material. An elastic material can be stretched or squashed by a force, but returns to its original shape and size when the force is removed. The metal in a wire or spring is an example of an elastic material. A weighing machine uses a spring. When an object is put on the weighing machine it is the pull of gravity that changes the spring's shape.

Why elastic springs back

When a force pushes or pulls on an elastic material, a strain force develops inside the material which acts in the opposite direction. If the pushing or pulling force is removed, the strain force pushes or pulls the material back into its original shape. An elastic material obeys Hooke's law.

Hooke's Law

Robert Hooke was an English scientist who lived 300 years ago. He performed experiments on wires and springs. He found that when a mass was added to a wire, the weight of the mass pulled the wire so that it stretched a certain amount. Through further experiments Hooke found that the wire or spring stretched in proportion to the mass hanging on it. His observations became known as Hooke's Law. This discovery allowed people to compare the weights of objects. For example, an object with a large weight stretched a wire or spring to a greater extent than an object with a small weight.

► Hooke's Law: the object with the larger mass stretches the spring more than the object with the smaller mass.

pointer

scale to measure extension

0

20 mm

small mass

58 mm

large mass

Measuring force

A **newton** meter is a device for measuring force. It contains a spring that can be stretched and a piece of metal to prevent it being stretched beyond its elastic limit. A pointer is attached to the bottom of the spring, and as the spring is stretched the pointer moves over the scale.

When the stretching force is balanced by the strain force the spring stops extending and the pointer shows the strength of the force on the scale. Forces are measured in units called newtons. You pull with a force of one newton when you peel a banana.

A newton meter could be used to measure the pulling force of this competitor as he pulls a jumbo jet 25m along a runway at Sydney Jet Base.

Change your planet to lose weight

Your mass is the amount of matter from which you are made. Your weight is the force with which you push down on the Earth. This force is due to the pull of gravity between you and the Earth. The force of gravity that exists between you and a planet depends on the size of the planet. **Mars** is smaller than the Earth and the force of gravity in its gravitational field is only one third that of Earth. This means that if you went to Mars your weight would be a third of the weight you are now! You would still be the same size because your mass would not have changed.

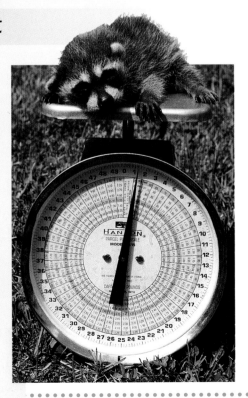

The mass of this opossum is squashing a spring inside the scales. A pointer attached to the spring has moved to show the opossum's weight.

Getting going

Isaac Newton was a scientist who lived 300 years ago and studied the way objects move. From his studies he set out three laws of motion. They describe how forces act and how objects behave when they are still or moving.

SCIENCE ESSENTIALS

Isaac Newton set out three laws of motion. They explain why things stay still or move.
An unbalanced force causes movement.
The speed of an object is the distance it moves in a certain amount of time. When an object increases its speed it **accelerates**.

Newton's three laws

Newton's first law: an object will stay still or keep moving steadily in a straight line unless an unbalanced force acts on it.

ball

space probe

Newton's second law: different sizes of forces produce different changes in an object's speed or in the direction it moves.

Newton's third law: when a force acts in one direction another force acts in the opposite direction.

When you are doing nothing

When you sit still, the downward force of your **weight** on the chair is balanced by the upward force of the chair and ground beneath it. By sitting still in your chair you are following part of Newton's first law of motion, which states that a body will stay still unless it is acted upon by an unbalanced force. Following the same law of motion, your body will start to move when an unbalanced force acts on it. That force will most probably be generated by your muscles when you decide to move or get up, although you could also be pulled or pushed out of the chair by someone else!

Making a move

When you prepare to rise from your chair, some of the muscles at the front of your body contract and pull on the upper part of your body. The muscles in your back relax and do not pull in the opposite direction. The unbalanced force makes you rock forward. More unbalanced forces pulling on your legs and arms raise you from your chair.

Acceleration

The distance a moving object covers in a certain amount of time is called its speed. When an object begins to move or increase its speed it is said to **accelerate**. A force pushes it forward. If you were driving in a motorbike race you would keep increasing the size of the forward force as you raced down the track. You would be following Newton's second law of motion. By increasing the force on your bike you would be making it increase its speed or accelerate. If you could make your bike accelerate better than your rival you would win the race.

▶ This test pilot shows how strong forces push on the face during rapid acceleration such as in a spacecraft launch. When the acceleration decreases, the forces weaken and his face returns to normal.

◀ The forward force generated by these bikes' engines make them accelerate down the track.

Speed

As you run along at a steady pace you cover a certain number of metres every second. This distance per second is called your speed. The speed of something can be measured in other units besides metres per second. A common unit for measuring speed is kilometres per hour.

SCIENCE ESSENTIALS

Speed is a measure of how far an object moves in a certain time.
Nothing travels faster than the speed of light. Sound travels more slowly than light.
Radar can be used to measure the speed of an object.

Measuring speed

The speed of an object is the measure of how long it takes to travel a certain distance. The object has to be moving steadily before the measurement can be made. When you run a 100-metre race you **accelerate** away from the start and then run as fast as you can. The time you take to cover this distance is not your speed because for part of the race you were accelerating.

To measure your speed over 100 metres you should be running as fast as you can when you pass the start line and keep running just as fast until you pass the finish line. In the same way, when a speed record is being attempted by a car or boat it must be going as fast as it can when it starts the measured distance it has to travel.

Shock waves can be seen blowing dust into the air on either side of the car as it reaches the speed of sound during the Thrust team's attempt at the land speed record.

The fastest thing in the Universe

Light travels at about 300,000 kilometres per second or 10,800,000 kilometres per hour. Scientists believe that nothing travels faster than light. Light that leaves the Sun in the direction of the Earth takes eight minutes to get here. The next nearest star to the Sun is called Proxima Centauri. Light leaving this **star** takes four years and four months to reach us.

The speed of sound

Sounds are made by **energy** that moves through the air. The energy moves the air particles and makes them vibrate. These movements make sound energy pass through the air. Sound travels through warm air at about 340 metres per second or 1224 kilometres per hour. It travels more slowly in cooler air, and in the cold air 10 kilometres above the Earth it travels at 1080 kilometres an hour.

When cars or aircraft travel at the speed of sound they make a wave of air pressure called a shock wave. This makes a bang called a sonic boom.

Most aircraft which travel at the speed of sound fly at a high **altitude** to prevent the shock wave reaching the ground.

The speed of sound is used as a unit of measurement of aircraft speed. This unit is called the Mach number, after Austrian scientist Ernst Mach, who studied fast-moving objects. An aircraft travelling at the speed of sound is travelling at Mach 1; Concorde flies at Mach 2 – twice the speed of sound. Some military aircraft, such as the Blackbird in the US Air Force, can fly faster than Mach 3.

The speed trap

Cars, vans, trucks and motorbikes are fitted with speedometers. These let the driver know the speed of the vehicle so that they can keep within the relevant speed limit. The speed of traffic is checked by police who use a radar gun. The gun is pointed at a vehicle approaching the police officer and **radio waves** are fired. They travel through the air and strike the front of the approaching vehicle. The waves are reflected by the front of the vehicle and travel back to the gun where they are detected by a receiver. The time difference between sending the waves and receiving the reflected waves is used to measure the speed of any vehicle that the gun is pointed at.

▲ Speed traps are often set up on roads where motorists are tempted to break the speed limit.

Friction

You may think that the covers of this book are very smooth, but if you were to examine them with a microscope you would see that they are covered in tiny bumps or projections. Other surfaces that you might think are smooth, such as a polished table top, have microscopic bumps too. When two objects touch, the bumps on their surfaces stick together. If there is a push or pull on one of the objects that are in contact, the bumps that are stuck together resist these forces with a force called friction.

Two kinds of friction

If you put this book on a table and push the book very gently from one side, the book will stay in its place. The frictional force is strong enough to prevent its movement. This frictional force is called static friction, from the Greek word *stasis*, meaning 'stillness'. The frictional force is pushing in the opposite direction, and so balances the force you are exerting on the book. This follows Newton's third law of motion which states that when a force is exerted in one direction, a second force of equal size is exerted in the opposite direction.

If you push the book a little harder, some of the bumps no longer stick to each other and the book starts to move. Even at that moment there are a few bumps sticking together and a force called sliding friction is exerted against your pushing force. The force of this friction does not balance the one you are exerting however, and so the book moves.

Moving for ever

Out in space there is no friction to slow down a moving object. Once the object is given a push it will keep going. This is stated in the second part of Newton's first law of motion (see page 10). The moving object will not change speed, just as a stationary object on Earth will not move unless given a strong push. In 1971 a **space probe** called Pioneer 10 was launched from the Earth. Today it is beyond the edge of the **Solar System** and travelling at 15 kilometres per second, but even at this speed it will take over 80,000 years to reach another **star**.

Decreasing friction

If you push a heavy box across the floor, the force of friction between the box and the floor is great and the box is difficult to move. This force can be reduced by putting rollers under the box or putting the box on wheels. The rolling action of the wheels and rollers reduces friction and makes the box much easier to move.

Wax is a substance that is rubbed onto a surface to make it very smooth. The wax covers the bumps and stops them sticking to bumps on other surfaces.

When a liquid flows between two surfaces that are in contact, it moves some of the bumps apart. This reduces the number of bumps on the surfaces sticking together and makes the static and sliding frictional forces smaller.

Oil is used to reduce the friction between the moving parts in a car engine. It makes the engine run smoothly and stops the metal parts from wearing out.

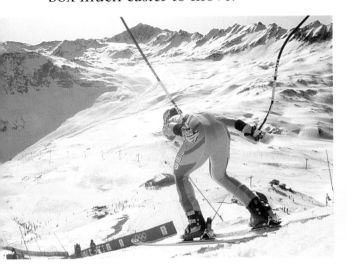

◄ Skiers wax their skis to reduce the friction between the skis and the snow so that they can travel faster.

Increasing friction

The soles of a hiker's boots have rough surfaces (a deep tread) to help increase friction and help him walk safely over various surfaces.

The tread of a tyre is designed to remove water from the surface of a wet road. It helps the surface of the tyre and the road to meet, so that friction can help the car grip the road and reduce the chance of skidding as the car slows down.

► Hikers' boots have a deep tread to increase the friction when they touch other surfaces. The friction between the boots and the ground prevents the hiker from slipping.

Air resistance

Air is made up from tiny particles called atoms and molecules. They move freely and push on any surface that they touch. When an object moves through the air the particles push against it. This pushing force is called air resistance. It slows down moving objects in the same way that **friction** does.

SCIENCE ESSENTIALS

Air resistance is a pushing force generated by air particles on a moving object.

A **streamlined shape** reduces air resistance on a moving object.

Air resistance acts in the opposite direction to **gravity** on a falling object. When the push of air resistance balances the pull of gravity, the falling object moves at a steady speed called the **terminal velocity**.

Feeling air resistance

If you keep your body low when you quickly pedal on a bicycle, you will begin to speed up. If you then sit up you will feel the push of air resistance on your face and body and you will begin to slow down.

The effect of streamlining

Air resistance can be reduced by making the shape of the moving object streamlined. A streamlined shape has curved surfaces over which the air particles can pass without pushing strongly. Cars are often designed with a streamlined shape. This means they are low at the front and high at the back, like a wedge. This wedge-shape cuts through the air more easily than the block-shape of a truck.

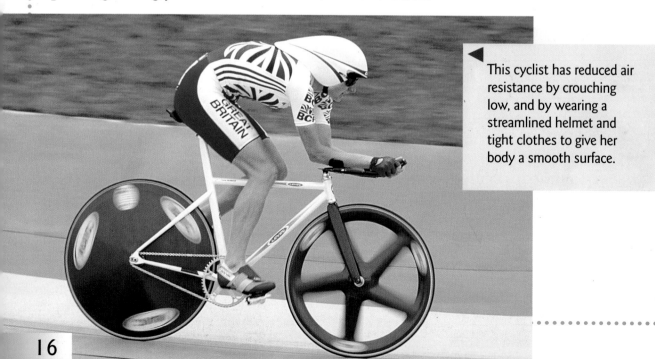

This cyclist has reduced air resistance by crouching low, and by wearing a streamlined helmet and tight clothes to give her body a smooth surface.

Diving through the sky

When **sky divers** jump out of an aeroplane, the pull of the Earth's gravity acts on their bodies all the way to the ground. At first this pull causes the sky diver's body to **accelerate** and they fall faster and faster to Earth, but as they fall, air resistance on their body increases and stops them **accelerating**. When this happens, the sky diver falls at a steady speed called the terminal velocity, which is about 60 metres per second.

Making a safe landing

If a sky diver hit the ground at 60 metres per second it would be the same as if they were travelling in a very fast racing car and hit a wall at 396 kilometres per hour. They would be killed instantly. Sky divers make sure that this does not happen by opening their parachutes when they are still far above the Earth. The parachute canopy has a very large surface, open to the air particles through which it rushes. The particles push up on the canopy and slow it down so that the diver can land without breaking a bone or spraining a joint.

Some animals which live in the rainforests of South East Asia have built-in parachutes. The flying squirrel has folds of skin along its sides which are also connected to its legs. When the squirrel jumps between trees, it stretches out its legs and the folds form a parachute.

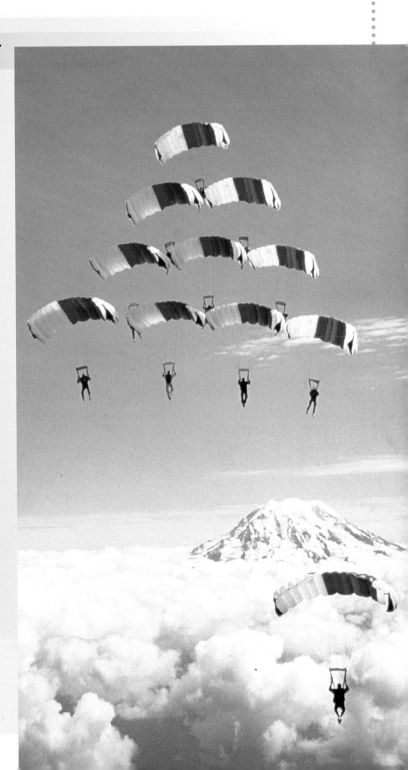

▶ When these parachutes were opened, the increase in air resistance slowed down the falling sky divers.

Going up, going down

A life boat is rushed down onto the sea and hits the water with a great splash but does not sink. A submarine slowly sinks beneath the waves to rise again hundreds of kilometres away. A hot-air balloon can rise high into the cold evening sky and descend later. These up and down movements are due to the way two **forces** oppose each other. The forces are **weight** and **upthrust**.

Why does a boat float?

When a boat is launched it pushes a volume of water out of the way to make room for the part of the hull that is below the water surface.
The water that has been pushed out of the way by the hull pushes back on the hull with a force called upthrust. If the upthrust is greater than the weight of the boat pushing down on the water, the boat floats. If the weight of the boat is greater than the upthrust, the boat sinks.

The upthrust of the sea water pushes on this tug boat and keeps it afloat.

How does a submarine sink and rise?

A submarine is equipped with **ballast tanks**. When the submarine is floating at the surface its ballast tanks are filled with air. At this time the upthrust is greater than the submarine's weight.

To get a submarine to dive, the crew fill its ballast tanks with water. The water increases the weight of the submarine so it is greater than the upthrust.

Later, when the crew need to get the submarine to rise, compressed air is used to push water out of the ballast tanks. This makes the upthrust greater than the weight of the submarine and so the submarine rises towards the surface.

Why don't we float in the air?

Upthrust force is produced by gases as well as liquids. Every object in air has an upthrust pushing on it. Your body pushes a volume of air out of the way to make a space for you to occupy.

The air you displace pushes back on you with a force of about 0.7 **newtons**. This is too small to balance the force of your weight which may be from 350–490 newtons.

The rise and fall of a hot-air balloon

When air inside a hot-air balloon is heated the air **expands**. Some of it passes out of the bottom of the balloon. The air remaining in the balloon has a smaller weight than the upthrust of the air around the balloon. This difference between the weight of the air in the balloon and the upthrust around it makes the balloon rise into the sky.

When the air in the balloon is allowed to cool down it **contracts** and more air is drawn in. The weight of the air in the balloon increases. When the weight is greater than the upthrust the balloon sinks to the ground.

► Upthrust around these balloons raises them hundreds of metres into the sky.

Pressure

If someone prods your arm you feel a pushing **force** over an area of your skin. When a force acts over an area in this way, pressure is created.

Studs and spikes

When you stand up you are in contact with the ground through the soles of your feet. Your feet cover an area of the ground and your body **weight** pushing down on the ground is spread out over this area. The pressure on the ground is not great enough for you to sink into the turf of a playing field. If you were to play a sport such as soccer or hockey on grass in ordinary shoes, your shoes would press down without entering the turf and you might slip if the grass was wet.

Shoes and boots for playing sports on grass have studs. When you wear them your weight presses down on a smaller area – the tips of the studs – and the pressure on the ground in those smaller areas is much greater. This increase in pressure pushes the studs into the turf so that your feet grip the playing field without slipping.

Sprinters have spikes on the soles of their shoes which create a great pressure, so their feet can grip the track while running fast.

When you skate on ice

Ice is an unusual solid. When it is squeezed very, very hard it turns into a liquid – water.

The blade on an ice-skating boot concentrates your weight onto a small area on the ice. When you set off across the ice, the pressure of your weight on the ice beneath the blade makes the ice melt. This means that when you skate you actually slide along on a **film** of water. As you move on and no longer press down on the ice it freezes again behind you.

Snow walking

When you stand on snow it pushes against the pressure of your feet. The pushing force of the snow is weaker than your weight and you may sink up to your knees in it! People who have to walk through snow wear snowshoes, which are like tennis rackets strapped to the feet. The large area of the snowshoe reduces the pressure of your body on the snow so that it matches the upward pushing force of the snow, and you do not sink.

► These snow shoes prevent the wearer sinking into the snow.

Air pressure

Air exerts a pressure all around us. We use air pressure to drink through a straw. When you suck on a straw you remove air from it, and so air can no longer push down on the drink inside the straw. The air pressure pushing down on the rest of the liquid surface pushes the drink into your mouth.

The pressure of air in the straw is the same as outside

The pressure of the air is less than outside

▲ When air pressure in the straw falls, the level of the drink rises.

Machines

We tend to think of machines as large noisy devices, yet most machines are much smaller and quieter than this. A machine is a device that makes a task easier to do. It does this by increasing the size of a **force**, changing the direction of a force or increasing the movement produced by a force.

SCIENCE ESSENTIALS

A machine makes work easier. It increases the size of a force, changes the force's direction or increases the movement a force produces.
A **lever** is a simple machine. There are three types of levers. They vary in the position of the **pivot** and the places where the forces act. A 'moment of a force' is a turning effect the force produces.

The door machine

When you push down on a door handle you exert a force on it. Inside the handle is the pivot on which the handle turns. On the other side of the pivot there is a short bar which pushes against a strong spring to release the door catch. The handle, pivot and bar make up a simple machine called a lever. The lever increases your small pushing force on the handle into a large pushing force on the spring so that you can open the door easily.

Types of levers

The lever is one of the simplest machines that exists. There are three types or classes of lever. The force applied to them is called the **effort force** and the force they produce is called the **load force**. The places where the effort force and load force are applied are different in each type of lever, as the diagram below shows.

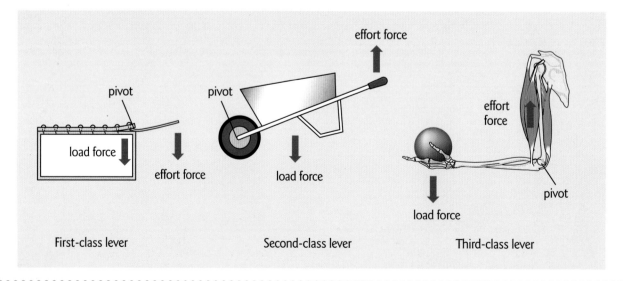

effort force

pivot

load force

effort force

First-class lever

pivot

load force

Second-class lever

effort force

load force

pivot

Third-class lever

Multipliers and magnifiers

In a first-class and second-class lever the effort force moves over a long distance and produces a larger load force which moves over a short distance. These classes of levers are called force multipliers.

▶ These machines are being assembled from smaller parts called components. Many of the components are simple machines like levers. The components work together to make a larger machine which performs a special task – like washing clothes.

In a third-class lever the large effort force moves over a short distance and produces a smaller force which moves over a longer distance. This class of lever is called a distance magnifier.

Just a moment

Although a force acts in a straight line, it can produce a turning movement. The turning effect is called the moment of the force. For example, when a spanner is used to release a nut, a **clockwise** moment may be produced. The moment of a force not only depends on the strength of the force, but also on the distance of the force from the pivot. On a see-saw, the pivot is in the middle. The moments of the forces pushing down on one side of the see-saw's beam are clockwise, while the moments of the forces on the other side of the beam are **anticlockwise**. If two people of the same weight sit at the same distance on either side of the pivot, the two moments are the same and the see-saw balances. If one person moves closer or further away from the pivot, the see-saw tips because the moments are no longer balanced.

◀ This mechanic is applying turning movements with the spanners to tighten the nuts on this car.

Magnetic forces

Magnets are fascinating because they exert forces on magnetic materials without touching them. The size of a magnetic force is strongest close to the magnet and gets weaker as the distance from the magnet increases.

The first magnets were discovered over two thousand years ago. They were black rocks containing iron, which were named magnetite. The country where they were found was called Magnesia which is now part of Turkey.

Magnetic materials

A magnetic material is made from one or more of four metals – iron, steel, cobalt and nickel. It can be made into a magnet which will exert a magnetic force on other magnetic materials. Some materials such as paper, wood and pottery are not affected by magnetic forces. A magnetic force can pass through this type of non-magnetic material and act on magnetic material on the other side. For example, a magnet on the front of a refrigerator door can hold note paper and post cards in place because its magnetic force pulls it close to the steel door.

The magnetic field

A magnet exerts a magnetic force in the space around it. The force is strongest close to the **magnetic poles** (at each end) and weaker further away. The space around a magnet in which the magnetic force acts is called the magnetic field. When a magnetic material enters a magnetic field, a magnetic force acts on it.

▶ If **iron filings** are sprinkled on paper and a magnet is placed on the sheet, the magnetic forces pull the filings into lines around the magnet. These lines of force show how far the force field extends around the magnet.

Pointing north and south

If a magnet is hung from a thread it will swing about and then settle with one end pointing north and the other end pointing south. The end pointing north contains the north-seeking pole of the magnet. The end pointing south contains the south-seeking pole. The magnet lines up this way because the inside of the Earth generates a magnetic field. The field seems as if it is produced by a huge bar magnet inside the Earth, but it is believed to be due to the way iron and nickel move at the Earth's core as the planet spins.

The pushing, pulling poles

If two magnets are brought together with their north-seeking poles (or their south seeking-poles) facing each other they will push each other apart. The like poles repel each other. If one magnet is turned round so that the north-seeking and south-seeking poles are together, the magnets will attract each other. Opposite poles attract each other.

Electricity and magnetism

When a current of electricity flows through a wire it creates a magnetic field. If the wire is made into a coil it behaves like a magnet when electricity passes through it. A magnet made in this way is called an electromagnet and is used in such devices as door bells and **security locks** on doors.

Levitation

This monorail train in Sydney, Australia, is a maglev train. This type of train uses electromagnets to make it move. There are electromagnets in both the train and the track. As the train moves along, electricity is passed through the train's electromagnets. The electromagnets on the track repel those on the train. This **repulsion** makes the train rise and **levitate** above the track. A second set of electromagnets on the track and train attract each other to pull the train along.

The electric motor

The electric motor was invented following the study of how **magnets** and wires carrying electricity push and pull on each other. There are two magnets in an electric motor. One is a permanent magnet, the other is an electromagnet. The movement produced in the electric motor is due to the pushing and pulling forces which the two magnets exert on each other.

SCIENCE ESSENTIALS

An electric motor contains a permanent magnet and an **electromagnet**. Magnetic forces between the two magnets make the motor produce a turning action. Electric motors have many uses.

The magnetic sandwich

In an electric motor the coil of wire is sandwiched between the north and south pole of the permanent magnet. The coil is attached to a rod and can spin round. When the coil spins, the rod spins too. The spinning end of the rod can be connected to other parts of a machine to make a useful force that will spin a wheel or turntable.

rotation produced   pivot

coil

magnet

N

S

rod

split ring (commutator)

carbon brushes

▲ ▶
This diagram shows the essential parts of an electric motor. Inside the motor shown in the photograph (right), the coil, magnet and rod are easy to see.

Switch on ...

In the motor the ends of the wire in the coil are attached into an electric circuit by a device called a **commutator**. When the current is switched on the electricity flows in one direction through the commutator and the coil. This makes the coil into an electromagnet. The north (and south) poles of the electromagnet are attracted to the south (and north) poles of the permanent magnet. These forces of attraction make the coil turn.

As the opposite poles come to face each other, the commutator switches the direction of the current through the coil. This reverses the poles of the electromagnet and they are now repelled by the poles of the permanent magnet. The forces of repulsion make the coil move again. As the electromagnet's poles keep changing, they push and pull on the poles of the permanent magnet and keep the rod spinning.

Motors at work and in your home

When you dry your hair with a hair dryer or clean your teeth with an electric toothbrush you are using an electric motor. A motor spins a compact disc or pulls the tape in an audio or video cassette. A motor provides the power to circulate the coolant in a refrigerator to keep your food fresh and turns the whisks in a food mixer. The turntable in a microwave oven is spun by an electric motor and your clothes are washed as they are tumbled by an electric motor in a washing machine.

▼

This locomotive picks up the electric current from an overhead cable through the metal structure called a **pantograph** on the locomotive's roof. The huge electric motor in the locomotive produces a force strong enough to pull a train weighing hundreds of tonnes.

Time to stop

When a moving object slows down it is said to **decelerate**. If the object is allowed to continue decelerating it will eventually stop.

The push of friction

If you kick a ball, it rolls along the ground. **Friction** acts on the parts of the ball that are touching the ground. This **force** pushes in the opposite direction to the way the ball is rolling. If the ball does not receive another kick it continues to decelerate and then stops.

The tired arrow

People in ancient times used to think that when an arrow was shot from a bow, the air that was pushed out of the way by the arrow rushed to the back of it and pushed it forwards. They believed that the arrow slowed down and fell to the ground when the air was tired of pushing it. They did not know that the arrow fell due to the force of **gravity**, and decelerated due to the push of **air resistance**.

Putting on the brakes

Almost every vehicle with wheels is fitted with **brakes**. The brakes are made from blocks or pads of tough material that can be pushed against a part of the wheel. On a bicycle the brake blocks push against the wheel rim; on a car there are pads which press on a disk around the wheel hub. Brakes are operated by **levers** (see page 22), like those on a bicycle's handlebars or a pedal in a car.

When someone puts on the brakes, the blocks or pads are pressed onto the wheel so that friction is increased and the bicycle or car decelerates.

▼ To turn corners, rally drivers have to slow down their cars within seconds, but if they slam on their brakes too hard they skid off the track.

Slowing down safely

A driver cannot stop a vehicle immediately. First the driver has to think about stopping. During this time the vehicle continues at its normal speed. The distance covered by the vehicle in this time is called the thinking distance.

When the driver has thought about stopping, the brakes are then applied. This causes the vehicle to decelerate and eventually stop. The distance covered by the vehicle while it slows down, until it stops, is called the braking distance. These two distances are added together to make the total stopping distance. For example, a car travelling at 48 kilometres per hour travels 9 metres while the driver thinks about braking, and 14 metres while the driver applies the brakes – making a total stopping distance of 23 metres. The lengths of these distances increase as the car goes faster or if it travels on a wet road.

Exploring space safely

By studying the laws of forces and **motion** we have devised many ways to start objects moving, control their speed and stop them safely. However, we live on an object – the Earth – which does not have any brakes. It is pulled round the Sun by the force of gravity. All the other objects in the **Solar System** are also moved by gravitational forces and can only be stopped when they collide into something else. If you look at a full Moon through a telescope you can see craters where large chunks of rock have crashed into its surface long ago when the Solar System was forming.

In spite of the problems of gravitational forces, we are able to construct **space probes** that can reach and explore other planets. We apply our knowledge of forces and motion in the planning and construction of these spacecraft so that they will travel safely through space and land on other worlds.

▼ This is an artist's impression of how a space probe will land on another planet.

29

Glossary

accelerate   increase in speed

air resistance   the push of air on a moving object

altitude   the height of an object in the sky

anticlockwise   curved direction opposite to that taken by the hands of a clock on a clock face

ballast tank   container on a submarine which is used to hold air or water

black hole   region of space which has such a strong **gravitational force field** that light cannot escape from it

brake   device to make a vehicle slow down and stop

clockwise   curved direction taken by the hands of a clock on a clock face

commutator   device which allows electricity to reach the coil in an electric motor

contract   become smaller and occupy less space

decelerate   decrease in speed

effort force   a force applied to a lever to oppose a **load force** and create movement

electromagnet   device which becomes a magnet when electricity passes through it

energy   a property of something which allows it to do work, such as move an object

expand   increase in size and occupy more space

film   thin layer of a substance

force   a push or pull which can change the movement of the shape of an object.

friction   the force which exists between two objects that are touching when a pushing force is applied to one object

galaxy   large group of **stars**

gravitational force field   region around a large object, such as a planet, where its gravity pulls on other objects around it.

gravity   **force** of attraction which exists between any two objects in the **Universe**

iron filings   tiny particles of iron that are produced by rubbing a piece of iron with a file

lever   a simple machine which enables a small force to produce a large amount of work

levitate   rise above ground and float at a certain distance above it

load force   a force executed by an object on a lever. This force is overcome by the application of an effort force.

magnet   metal object that can attract and repel other magnets and can attract unmagnetized metals such as iron and steel

magnetic pole   region in a **magnet** where the magnetic force is very strong

Mars   planet next to the Earth – its **orbit** is further from the Sun than the Earth's

mass   the amount of matter in an object, or a substance such as water or air

Milky Way Galaxy   the galaxy which contains the solar system

moon   rocky object that moves around a planet

motion process in which an object changes position

newton unit used for measuring **forces**, just as seconds are used to measure time

orbit path of a planet or comet around a star, or a moon around a planet

pantograph device on a locomotive with an electric motor for collecting electricity from overhead cables

pivot place or an object on which something turns

pulse movement of a particular type of blood vessel (called an artery), caused by the action of the heart

radar (short for **ra**dio **d**etection **a**nd **r**anging) a system that uses **radio waves** and their reflections to detect objects

radio waves waves that have electrical and magnetic properties, such as light waves and microwaves. Radio waves can be made to carry instructions to make sounds and pictures in a television set.

repulsion pushing apart of two objects, usually due to a magnetic force

security lock a lock on the door of a public building such as a school which is opened by a security officer or by pressing buttons on it in a particular sequence, rather than by using a key. They often contain electromagnets.

shock wave wave of air of a different pressure to the surrounding air; shock waves travel away from a fast-moving object

sky diver person who falls a long way through the air for pleasure before opening their parachute

Solar System the Sun and its **orbiting** planets, moons and comets

space probe device used to investigate objects in the **Solar System** and beyond

star huge ball of gas in which hydrogen gas changes to helium gas with the release of light and heat.

streamlined shape shape that passes easily through air or water

submarine a vessel which can travel under water. It is used for military purposes and may carry missiles and torpedoes and can stay under water for weeks. Small submarines which can only stay under water for short periods are called submersibles and are used for exploring the ocean.

terminal velocity the steady speed at which an object falls when the forces of **gravity** and **air resistance** are equal

tide the rise and fall of the sea-level on the shore

Universe the place in which we live. It is composed of space, stars, planets, moons and comets.

upthrust the upward force on an object which comes from the liquid or gas surrounding it

wax solid material made from chemicals in oil

weight the **force** with which an object pushes downwards on a planet or **moon**

Index